Blackdamp

Blackdamp

Poems by Michele Harris

David Robert Books

© 2019 by Michele Harris

Published by David Robert Books
P.O. Box 541106
Cincinnati, OH 45254-1106

ISBN: 9781625493088

Poetry Editor: Kevin Walzer
Business Editor: Lori Jareo

Cover Photo: Suzanne Harris

Visit us on the web at www.davidrobertbooks.com

Acknowledgements

Grateful acknowledgement is made the following publications in which these poems first appeared:

Anatomy & Etymology: "Avondale Mining List" and "Moon
    Jellyfish"
Anderbo: "The Highway Behind Her"
Cicada: "Petrichor: After Earl Grey"
The Columbia College Literary Review: "Scraping Clean" and
    "The Architect"
Cosumnes River Journal: "Saving Things"
Dirtflask: "Morgue A" and "The Aquarium"
Eclectica: "The Johnstown Flood" and "The Mushroom Miner"
Escarp: "Parable" and "The Tines"
Falling Star Magazine: "Weeding"
New Millennium Writings: "Instinct"
Northridge Review: "Things You Can't Say"
Pigeon Bike: "Ribs"
The Prose-Poem Project: "How to Stay Under"
The Sheepshead Review: "Thread (Dream Poem #4)"
Snapdragon: A Journal of Art & Healing: "Elasticity"
Stirring: "Hypnagogia" and "Kinzu"
The Susquehanna Review: "Long Drive Home"
The Tishman Review: "Overdose" and "The Poison Place"
Turbulence: "Between Briars"
Uncanny Valley: "Pymatuning Spillway"

To everyone who has opened up new places in the world that I didn't know existed before:

to Matt, whose love inspired every bit of light in this book.

to Lloyd Schwartz and Joyce Peseroff, without whom this manuscript would not be possible.

to my parents, who cultivated an early love affair with books.

to my sister, who captured the heart of my book in photograph.

to Marsha Steiner Fox, who helped me fall in love with language at a time when I had trouble loving myself.

to Rachel, who shares my love for adventure, and language, and cold-nosed dogs.

to Danielle, who sipped Turkish coffee with me on Sundays while breaking, unbreaking, and polishing poems.

to all my wonderful friends, family, teachers, OLLI students. I am so lucky to know you all, and my life is so much brighter because of it.

Contents

ONE

Bildungsroman

Dodging trucks in vapor trails
of dust, we trekked back roads, we were twelve,
we were alone with the gravel crackling
under us up Bowser's hill. Angie,
now dead, snapped a stalk of shattercane,
slipped it between her lips, and with a quick click
of her thumb, lit it: a dozen winged ants
poured out in her spit. How we walked
to Kelly's house, her windows filled
with strung up bed sheets, her Stepdad
patting her down, reaching into her blouse
to pull out a pack of Marlboro lights.
How I unrolled my sister's hunter green
sleeping bag in the woods beside Camilla Brink
in her wide pink rimmed glasses
when she told me how bad it hurt
getting her cherry popped.
And I didn't say a thing.
Because I didn't know what that meant.
And in a year's time,
how her flat belly would swell
until she disappeared
from school. Angie unzipping her bag, hands
clutching the purple nylon knuckle-hard,
twisting it, rehearsing
for the steering wheel, the loose screeching
brakes, the oak tree in Sligo.
How we felt mosquitos whirring around us
like stars, how we even felt the stars

rising like bugs, their silent hulls
winging the sky, and the next day
before our parents took us
home, when we walked and talked
and smoked, the sun
lit the tip of the sky, the stars
poured out.

Overdose, December 23
for Sam, 1986-2013

I still think of you with blood
in your teeth, staining

the playground's asphalt.
Third grade, kickball

in the outfield, and you bounding up
to stop a home run, your open mouth

colliding with the metal lip
of the dumpster. I laughed

because I didn't know
you were hurt. Then blood,

the nurse, your front teeth
shattered out of your jaw.

For a week, you disappeared
from class. When you came back,

I was amazed at your two-toned
smile, the knocked-out teeth

magically remade:
the sometimes quickness

of healing. That first day back
you slept the whole bus ride

home, winding through miles
of abandoned farmland,

slag heaps, the unrelenting
orange mouths of wildflowers.

November 12th on Fenneltown Road

A Lyndora man died at midnight. I listened
to sirens announcing enough smoke

two stations had to slough off flames
tonguing the triple decker's top floor.

It must have burned through the water
in his eyes. And the only picture

in *The Leader Times* showed singed roof, sucked out
windows, and the red downstairs door

where his shrieking
neighbors had escaped, where two small, faceless

pumpkins freeze on his porch.

Saving Things

Blood, so little of it—a thud
against our sunflower yellow shutters.
My Uncle and I craned necks

to the gravelly weeds, outskirts
of our driveway, where a winged thing
twitched among the Bunsen flames

of thistle bulbs: Bird, no—bat, the tip
of his right wing bent backward,
cobwebbing threads of bone.

Kneeling, I ripped a stalk
of grass, and feathered it
over the good wing. It straightened

then shut like an accordion.
I dreamed of sneaking sticky fruit
to our root cellar, tweezing

dead moths by their wings
to keep him alive.
I still remember this feeling

breaking open
like the bat
under my Uncle's heel.

Between Briars

We sat where Grandpa's barn
burnt down, unsheathing kernels

of wild wheat, raw grain scattered
on our laps. My knee

was bleeding, and your spit
and palm smeared it clean.

Wheat rustling off our shorts,
we trampled thickets, tweezed

raspberries between briars.
Smoke corkscrewed from the Flicks'

burn barrel. Mosquitoes whirred
about the jagged pond,

whined in our ears.
On the way home, your foot

caught on a muck rake
sunk in mud: five

rusted prongs straining up
where you fell

chest-first,
eyes bulging wide.

Before your Mom found me huddled
and howling in high grass, I picked

a tick off your wrist, gripped
your hand, rust

under your fingernails.

Hatching

Staring between the webbed toes
of my Frogger night light, I dreamed

of tadpoles, their bulbous
bodies bursting

arms and legs. Sometimes,
I'd draw these dreams, breaking

chartreuse crayons. I left
water in a bucket on our back porch.

I prayed for eggs.
In a few days, the bucket filled

with tiny, finless bodies
whipping their backsides

into the soft current. My Mom
refused to tell me, so my Dad

flipped the bucket
over the side of the deck,

wondering how soon
their question mark bodies

would have sprouted wings,
thoraxes, a stinging

taste for skin, while I stood
behind the porch screen and cried

for the tadpoles that weren't tadpoles.

How to Stay Under

They had me climb in the bathtub. It wasn't really a bathtub. Tubs are supposed to be in bathrooms, where you can close the door. It was cold. The tile was the color of mint bubble gum. Pastor Whelan was in there, too, wearing some kind of robe. I didn't get a robe. I was in a turtleneck that pressed into my throat. He was talking to the church from a microphone, angled to catch his voice by the tub. I'd never seen a microphone near a tub before. Sometimes in his hot tub, Uncle Sonny would sing Billy Joel songs into his beer cans. His favorite was Piano Man, where he'd mime a harmonica by his mustache. And whistle, which I hated. Once he sang about all the lights in New York City going out. Dad said it was about the end of the world. I closed my eyes and tried to imagine that. My palms skimmed the tub water. Pastor Whelan put his thumbs on my shoulders, pushed until water rushed over my head, made my ears sound like fists pressed into them. I didn't know how long to stay under. I pretended I was made of fire. I pretended this would put me out.

1996: the holes

in my ears are thumbed
shut, my Dad's plaid arms

slung around a rifle. Mom
shivers on our deck,

her freshly scabbed
forearm in a bandage.

A whole world can fit
in the scope of a gun:

this one is startled
peach fur, aqua-eyed,

nuzzling a stuffed mouse.
The gunshot stuns

the air—the stray lunges
away, bolts deep into woods,

as if the shot had missed.

Parable

After the yelling, I hid every spoon we had. At dinner, we sipped tomato soup off forks. The next day, I learned to hide the belts.

Pymatuning Spillway, Pennsylvania

1.

Fifty cents will buy you a loaf of bread
to hock into this lake.

Already, moldy slices are fishtailing
in the current, where thousands

of fat carp muscle
the water open.

Air screams in their gills
as they open themselves

to thick scraps that bob,
bubble, and vanish.

2.

You spilled dozens
of back roads behind you

so your children could lob
stale bits of bread

into the spillway, watch carp
flap and writhe,

slap against their own bodies,
make the green water boil.

3.

These fish know you:
the chance of crumbs

worth more to them
than breathing. Empty-bagged,

you drive your kids home
to their mother's house, your face cut

by headlights, your life the same
possibility of bread.

Crabgrass

1.

Someone dragged the dog's body into a hole, ripped
thick into red clay, a day's

worth of digging. Someone
guided the bullet

that bit into his cheek.

2.

Aspergillosis, ceaseless sleep-
halting yowls, stray turned pet,

and they regretted it.

3.

It was a shot
of Nembutal to the neck or .22 to his snout.

My parents spared
the vet bill.

4.

Standing on the stained deck, I stare into the peeling green
box he slept in, water bowl spilling

with leaves, the slack, rust-knotted chain
still coiled in crabgrass.

The Tines

of my Grandma's blue-
veined hands vanish
into mine

Sometimes rain grips the trees
like this

TWO

Growing up Thin

I'd have trekked Redbank creek by boat
with a bottle of rum and a boy thumbing
and tonguing my blue bikini top
off into the crabgrass.

I'd have still pinched at my hips
and wished for less.

I'd have a baby I'd hold
tight in my gut
until, unbreathingly,
I would dissolve
its neurons out of me.

I'd have still hated the way men looked at me
but for other reasons.

Deleterious Mutation BRCA2 9927del14

White-gloved and needle-fisted
they'll search me tomorrow,
strain their eyes at the ancient scrawling

under my skin, looking for a misprint.
They will read me like a fortune cookie—
cracking open letters to spell

odds: *ovarian, uterine, cervical, breast,*
throat, stomach, skin.
The worst case is a prophecy

to fulfill. I won't undo the infinitesimal
mistakes my body makes, replicating
error after error, until a knot

ripens inside me, until I ready myself
for years of being a woman and learning
to lose all that makes me so.

Catechetics

And so preserves me that
without the will of my Father in Heaven,
not a hair can fall from my head.
-Creeds of Christendom

Bleached flax molts
from my mother's skull, falls
by the fistful.

Treatment is fast
and severe; spoke-thin
bones poke at her

translucent
skin, the curves
dissolved away.

After three months,
she blames God
for nothing,

begs me
to keep her
in my prayers.

Every night I pour
my clumsy words
into the darkness.

Every day she
pales a lighter white,
waning, or healing,

and all I'm left
to do is stomach
my anger, make

my hands wring
love from her
still breathing body.

Coupling

They're tossing pennies
down the storm drain

to pass time, Birch Street filled
with the tinging of copper

against the grating.
They are young, their hair

luminous black
like Lake Erie at night.

The sky opens.
Pigeons' feet curl

into their flown bodies.
The couple starts yelling.

Rain tongues the bus's roof,
rolling R's the way

I can't, echoing their fight
in Spanish: *las cervezas*,

el embarazo. Leaving,
the woman crushes the ribs

of her umbrella back into her bag.

Ribs

Knees wincing, he kneels
beside the broken-down Chevy he almost
gave up last year, the spit shine
of its China red lacquer, turtle wax and the tip
of his exposed finger skimming
where ribs would be if she
were a woman. Unlike a woman,
she doesn't run. He jimmies open the door. The radio
works. And when he gets inside, mint leather
stuck to his bare back, he thumbs over the knobs
just right until *I Fall to Pieces* juts on, slow
bass shuddering the dashboard, crawling
up the tented fabric of the car's roof,
Patsy Cline sirening
velvet and a soft
throb burrows in his throat.

Weeding

The soft singe of autumn: marigolds
and thistle rooting together in the pit
where his mother had kept
a garden. Yesterday he'd painted
the door Carolina blue and speared
two red and white signs into the lawn.
Today he edges into the back yard, examines
the tangle of straining vines, gray nubs of emptied
dandelions, flaking Gardenias. Bending, he pulls
with both gloved hands until the weedy spine
breaks free of the roots and throws it
aside. Next the tomatoes, stunted red
fruit knuckle-small, and snaps
them loose, the broken white threads
still funneling moisture up
to a phantom limb. Nothing is spared. He pulls
until blisters well beneath his yellow gloves,
blisters that redden and throb and will pop—
not today, but tomorrow
or next week, gripping a fork
or hammering a nail, one will burst and leak,
and the skin slack and half torn off
will petal off him.

Architect

First comes the skeletal rise:
steel shunting girders, glass

panes large enough to break
ten men. Palladian

windows, tympanum, green
kaleidoscope-glass. Elevators

chuting through like red
blood cells. Then comes the law

among all bodies whose spines
stick perpendicular to the horizon:

to survive in wind, sinews
must flex and sway, must give in

to their own trembling.

The Highway Behind Her

She drives to God
knows where, veers left onto 79,
watches exactly where this road

won't lead. City lights
starring her back, she cuts
a lane of traffic, pulls
into Al's Fresh Melons. Black coffee,
a pack of Newports, her husband's brand.
How smoke used to slip
out of his mouth, like words he meant
to take back—

the way the wind erases
its own work, rousing leaves
when yesterday it ripped them down.

THREE

Ars Poetica

I don't use a washcloth in the shower. It's probably bad for me.
Not exfoliating, I mean. I bet someone has died from it.
Somewhere, I read that dust is 70% skin, which means when you
walk into the room you grew up in, you are breathing yourself.
Last week I blew the dust off my bookshelf and rose by the
window in particulate, tumbling light.

Petrichor

I.

Today it rained, water spilling in a soft hiss.
Sun tongues the horizon.

Under our feet, leaves thumbprint the sidewalk orange-red.
They clot in storm drains, arterial.

In your eyes, there is bergamot.

Years ago, in the woods, we could smell storms
before they came. Ozone and moss.
The sky opening like a peony, my hair
wet in your eyes. Ankle-deep
in mud, we trudged home, wind
rustling the light until it fell.

II.

Your ambering laugh catches me
like a mosquito.

Your lungs are full of leaves, themselves
full of lungs, and we're watching them
stop breathing.

If we did this, we'd also turn blue, the moon
caught in our throats. Not sea-hued, but periwinkle.
As if we'd slept in snow.

We'd make human-shaped dents
and call them angels.
We'd build forts the sun
would turn to water.

There is snow, love, sleeping in us.
When you let go, it drifts.

Thread (Dream Poem #4)

To save it, the doctors sewed another heart to mine.
I didn't know whose.
They popped my sternum
with a deep needle, and pulled
me open like a crab.

You kiss me awake
and I touch your beaming crooked smile.
Behind my stapled purple skin
I hope this heart
your green eyes revive
is still mine.

A Catalogue of Teeth

1.

28, small-mouthed, teeth corseted
in braces, gum-hanging
a yellow-white enameled chandelier
at times, forgotten
by toothbrushes. If only
you were quiet enough, listened enough
to sometimes hide them.

2.

28, 5 molar fillings, chipped bicuspid,
nicotine-sunny. A slight yellow like the cusp
of egg-white on yolk. The way, when you laughed,
your eyes crinkled
until they disappeared in your face.
The way you disappeared
like the slight spittle from your lips
on my cheek, evaporating.

3.

32, 9 fillings, cracked molar, two crowns.
You with your immigrant teeth.
I see you in an old Czech film, *Ostře
sledované vlaky*, your mouth chewing
another language. Your skin luminous
silver—love, how I would die

to describe the gray
of your eyes set in black and white.

Meanings

I'm afraid to look up
certain words.
They don't
always mean
what I need them to.
Like *saturnine*,
inflammable,
embarazada. Or
muckle, as in
muckle-mouthed.
I thought it meant lightly
pursed, the curve
of one jewel
red half
beaming
open.
Now there's
no word
for the way
your lips look
when you're inches
from my face
and whispering.

Things You Can't Say

Sometimes I call a fire truck red, not gum red or rhubarb red or
red like the nub in the corner of your eye, really, it's fire truck red,
but you can't call it that, just like you can't say a river is wide as a
river, or a needle is sharp as a needle and doomed for a haystack
where sharpness doesn't matter anyways because hay is soft if
bristly and buries deep, hides things you shouldn't step on like
horseshit cowshit or especially *pigshit*, hides sight but not scent
so learn to walk by smell alone and don't dare tell a woman her
neck smells like a begonia or worse, a rose, don't say as she
opens her mouth her lips are red blooms because the more a
flower opens the more it can't stop, don't talk about your body
as an *anther* or she'll assume you have a lisp, don't bring up
pollen or bees because why mention things that sting, and when
she pushes her chest against yours don't talk about pistils or
you'll start holding her like one.

The Tuesday Before Our Anniversary

A first date: the couple beside us
fumble tongues while thumbing
the menu, hands tightening

around their Miller Lights.
Calamari comes, then a Reuben, fries.
They swap bites, Russian

dressing beading on her bangs.
A thread of sauerkraut drops
down her blouse, deep down, where two

red acrylic nails tweeze it out.
We pull on coats, unroll
a careful number of bills,

leave without talking. They're still starving
for what's not even hinted
at under clothes: a phoenix

tattoo, a birthmark shaped like Florida, hair
where there also might not be hair—
the one-armed car ride home, the impossibly slow

unlocking of the dead bolt door, the final clack
of the futon as it goes from couch to bed.

Save Yourself

Drive alone. Better yet, don't
drive, but know walking
has risks.

Avoid stairs: certain steps
are waiting to be missed.

Don't eat anything
with bones. Chew
thirty times before swallowing.

On icy streets, beware
of kisses. There's potential
for more than just a prayer
to leave your lips.

Venice Sinking

Presents a business opportunity
for submarine gondoliers, their arias
the same, but sea-warbled
while the ancient watery city
spheres along in one convex
rainbowy panorama, fish
flitting through
what used to be sky.

Fission

When we lip words

into each other, every vowel you whisper

comes out in my voice.

Inside us, microflora bloom,

split, and split again.

Inside, our blood unbluing (lung-

sung red) circles our centers, Ptolemaic.

Don't be afraid of bodies

you can't feel

swarming you: *Archaea,*

Sarcina, spinning

our skin's fissures: thigh to thigh

they multiply

and divide

the spaces between us.

Moon Jellyfish

"The chicken has an inside and an outside. Remove the outside
and you find the inside. Remove the inside and you find the
soul."
-Paul, Vivre sa vie

Lit like firing neurons, they drift

in the bubbling current, closing

and opening. Translucent

wombs, bellying water

behind glass. Each tentacle

finer than an eyelash.

Rip back their skin

with your eyes. If they had hearts,

you'd see them beat and punch

out blood. But they don't hide

what they are: diaphanous

bell, velarium, nerves and water,

this water—if you believed

in a soul, it'd be here: *this*

is what moves them, fills them,

drowns inside them.

The Poison Place

"You who have proved
how much like me you are:
how could I trust you?"
- *James Richardson*

I.

I find you mouth-down
in the bathroom, your body

crumpling after your heart
rate plunged, blood turned

sludge in your veins.
The sound the floor made

when the force of your body hit it.
My thoughts run to lye,

bleach, diazepam,
but it's an accident,

syncope, your vasovagal nerve
strummed just right,

and you wake up
sore and thirsty.

II.

Charges for sapphire
lace lingerie, silk Cuban

heel stockings, stilettos,
for a woman I'll never meet.

You tell me it's fraud,
and, *love*, it is.

III.

Whispered midnight hotlines:
ringing up strangers

who strain to hear
every solicitous way

you've considered slipping
out of your bones.

IV.

When you're late from work
I wonder if this will be the night.

Would I go to the office
the next day, when they're searching

for you? I'm ashamed
that I might.

V.

It is terrifying
not knowing when
this poem is going to end.

FOUR

The Aquarium

I.

Before she died, the albino catfish
emptied her body of eggs,

hundreds of them pimpling
the tank's glass, milky white,

the water barely cooler
than blood. After birth, she'd grown

spores in her belly
that cysted over then burst.

The mother gone, the cherry barbs
and neon tetras prodded

each egg until it broke, the tank
pockmarked with torn open blisters.

II.

A Tigerfin guppy shoots tiny white fish
after fish out of her, a live birth.

In minutes thirty mouths
writhe in the breeding tank

like larvae. When the mother guppy
is empty, she follows

their tiny eyes and shut fins
and swallows each one whole.

When another baby
disappears in her

mouth, the others
don't dart off.

There is a kind of love
in how she buries her young

inside her. There is a love
when they let her.

Elasticity

If someone entered my mind, a bed
of *Taraxacum*, shrieked loose your stem and coughed

away its cobwebbed clock, there'd be no evidence
I loved you. You turned everything

into a game: work was hide-and-seek, shrinking
days in the tight belly of your apartment.

Your friends
loosened from you like teeth, or your first set

of plastic jacks, loved
to breaking.

I was a favorite:
a spaldeen to pop

against a brick wall,
bucking between

the concrete kiss
of bricks, the cold

softness of your open hands.

Long Drive Home

When I told you I was in love
with someone else, you promised
to leave me burning

in the August heat,
car idling,
your mouth half-shut.

Instead, asphalt tumbling
behind us, you drove
until the sun

was the only thing around us
we could recognize.
You drove until our faces

were wet and raw,
until our voices
were ground to grit.

The car swerved right.
You pulled off and wrenched
me against you, hard

enough to hurt. We kissed
and I felt nothing
except the solid warmth

of your arms, eyes dimmed,
our bodies once more
unraveling one into the other.

Lost in our mouths,
in wordless language,
I tried to imagine

that the hard vowels
you kept breathing into me
weren't his.

New Year's Eve

When the phone rang, your hello
hit me like confetti. I stooped
over the neighbor's steps, receiver tight
to my ear like a conch, half expecting
to hear the ocean: water weighed down
with salt, the suck of surf, sand
slipping under (the way taffeta
slides off a woman's hips),
the sea ebbing, ebbing out.
In the morning when I woke
beside him, reached for champagne
glasses, clouded and empty,
I understood the sound
was in my head
and it was blood.

The Evidence

Your freckled chest to mine, it's getting near
the time for me to vanish from your bed
and hide the proof that I was ever here.

Your wife due home at six, we sling our beers
at the blue bins and scramble for our shed
clothing. I promise this time's the last. Near

the window, sun ignites the bed, the hair
you peel off pillows in long, blonde threads
to hide the proof that I was ever here.

Don't blame me. It's not your first affair.
I'd have ended it the day our mouths first met
but you wrenched your chest to mine. And you were near

ready to leave her, but wedding rings will bear
ungodly weight before they buckle. Forget
my face, my kiss, the proof that I was here,

the seven months it's taken me to fear
the sting of your skin, your eyes on me like lead.
Bury me in your chest, or somewhere near.
Destroy the proof that I was ever there.

Clearing Away

The dishwasher runs cold, wineglasses stung
with soap scum, fusty sponges
wrung out with Dawn. I begin
the scrubbing away
of everything left
after you eat: tomato stains,
turmeric, the flaccid whites
of an egg. Then the bathroom,
the almost invisible
piss stains under the toilet,
and above, an orchid
blooming fuchsia,
sunburned by a south window,
fighting spider mites
who drape their softest webs
between the leaves,
the ruin
nearly microscopic.

Hypnagogia

1

Beside me you push out air
in chokes, ethyl strong.

I turn upside down
in bed, put my head

towards your bare feet. You bleat
the air in coughs and snores, kick

and turn in your sleep, thrashing
to breathe.

2

Your fingernails turned lithium-white,
lunula gone, the half moons

emptied out of you. Your scabbed
legs, your stomach that holds

nothing down, even the way
you shake means something.

Your musty kiss that goes
no further. You will stop

61

me from speaking of it:
something inside you

scars and swells and something
inside me shrinks and shrinks.

3

I walk until roads recede
and all is black dirt, bramble, veins

of trampled grass, and flowers inching up
under bald patches of sky, where light trickles

its yellow into them: ox-eye, hooked
crowfoot, silverweed,

creeping buttercup, sickle
leaf golden aster, thin

leaved sunflower, chrome yellow,
urobilin bright. They, too, wait for your skin,

for the whites of your eyes
to burst into color.

Kinzu

Before the train churned across the 19th century
wooden bridge that shook and shrieked under it,

we got off, I was five, and we were going to watch
it ease along the crisscrossed splintery beams

that ran along the gorge like a thick stitch.
My Dad gave me a handful of pennies, all a deep rust

like the bottom of Bear Creek. One
a wheat penny: mottled green, powdery.

Because he said the train
would change them, I bent

and let five coins clink on the right side of the track.
After the train chugged by, slower

than we could walk, the bridge
shrugging under it, I scooped up the pennies,

each oblong and brassy,
sharp to the touch.

Years later, kneeling over the commuter rail
you would tell me that pennies

could derail a train. Of course a lie.
When later you empty the twelfth bottle

of the night I hear the hiss
of another opening, smell it, backwash

evaporating in empties—it is what a secret
smells like: sweet, like an almond

whiff of cyanide. Sweet like lilies at a wake.
It leaks from between your teeth, from the pores

on your neck. You reach for my copper
hair, pull me to you hard, and everything

I don't say
trembles like pennies on the tracks.

FIVE

Farmhouse

Maybe the smell of pine woke him, maybe dizziness, the rushed
thud in his chest, the burning hurt of his head, maybe the damp
outline of his own body beneath him, but he awoke, knew the
smell from the war, ripped away the sheets that clung to him, ran
for his empty paint bucket, its handle ringing like the tongue of a
bell as he dragged it across the splintery floor to the kitchen,
turned on the faucet, filling it not fast enough until he wrenched
it from the sink and ran to the living room whose floor planks
burned his feet and threw the bucket's water loose and in the
dense fog of steam there was only the sound of water hissing
across the floorboards.

Primigravida
for my great grandmother

When you buoyed and bulged inside your mother,

she was unmarried. She never married. Your father, who owned

the Gallitzin Hotel, put an icebox in the room

where they'd knocked you into being. She hoped that cell by cell

you'd drip out of her in sleep, that the swell and kick

of you would cease. Because you were born, she

tucked you beneath his last name.

The Johnstown Flood
for Ethel Fitzharris, Great Grandmother

You were two when the South Fork Dam
collapsed, when the flood thrust loose
every rail car and thread

of barbed wire from Cambria Iron Works.
Smoke leaked from burst open boilers. Oaks
and pines unfastened their roots, climbed

the current until they caught
against a house, and a barn, and a church.
Before the flood reached Iron Street

your mother had been pushing
a needle through the side
of a pleated cotton dress.

By the time she snapped you
in her arms, water climbed up
her elbows. Outside, timber

knocked and knocked. Clambering
to the attic, toeing bare boards, she pressed
you to her belly. The straining yowl

of house walls meant no going
back downstairs, where your grandfather
slept tossing about images

of Meath in his head: thistle
that infiltrated the tubers, that broke
through mud and leaf to creep

between the tilled rills of the soil, just
opening after a good rain.

MORGUE "A" – FOURTH WARD SCHOOL-HOUSE

after the Johnstown Flood

185. Von Alt, Henry.
    Collar-button and spoon.

146. Unknown.
    Said to have been Mary Hamilton or
    Miss Mollie Richards, but afterward
    found to be wrong.

20. Unknown.
    Hulbert House porter. Supposed to be
    William Henry. Colored. Valuables.

1. Hamilton, Miss Laura (Mary).
    Was to have been married on the next
    Tuesday. Body delivered to her brother.

39. Unknown.
    Burnt. Sex unknown.

18. Burns, John.
    Brakeman Cambria Iron Co. Left eye
    gone. Buried at "prospect," June 9.

76. Unknown.
    Female. Thirty years. Dark
    luxuriant hair.

86.   Unknown.
Male. Weight about 170. Height
about 5' 9''. Head burned off.
Dark lace shoes. Revolver and knife.

206.   Larimer, James.
Purse with one cent. Two keys. Two
knives.

193.   Brown, Miss Emily.
Of Woodvale. Removed. Ring
given to her sister. Little
girl baby in her arms when found.

136.   Shumaker, John S.
Son of James. Walter, Jennie and
Edith also drowned.

144.   (See No. 53.)

176.   Thomas, E.M.
All but hips and lower limbs
burned away. Bunch of keys with tag
marked E.M. Thomas. Gun screwdriver.
Pocketbook and buckeye.

240.   Female. Large. Full face, full lips,
small nose, light hair, pregnant. Key
and one cent.

135.   Deihl, Miss Carrie.
        Shippensburg, PA. Claimed by Wm.
        H. Ocker, of Philadelphia, to whom she
        was engaged to be married, and re-
        moved by him to be buried.

21.   Prosser, Fanny.
        Daughter of Charles Prosser, of Cresson.
        Earrings. Silver ring on middle finger
        of left hand. Can't get it off.

Disposal of the Dead
after the Johnstown Flood, 1889

Burying the dead meant unburying:
after the wreckage, even their houses had closed over them.
Retrieving bodies meant pulling, meant barbed wire
cutting through bone. It meant grasping arms
loosened from bodies, following whispers
of smoke at the Old Stone Bridge where the dead were heaped
over the dying. It meant softening screams with ether
when a woman's scalp was ripped from brow to neck.
It meant picking pockets or prying purpled lips
to count teeth when a face
couldn't call to mind a name, comforting
those who couldn't live
but did anyways. It meant holding breath
when wounds stitched shut
ripped back open.

Avondale Mining List

JONES, EDWIN D of Hanover. Head thrown back,
and tea-can slung around his neck. Found
among the sixty-seven. Wife.

HOWELL, Chern, name in illegible ink
on arm; two fingers off. Lived
at Walsh Hill, Plymouth. Wife and four
children. Eyes closed, mouth open.

REESE, DAVID, Jr., Plymouth (Coal Street). Father
and brother brought out dead. Mouth
all bloody; tongue between teeth. Single.

HATTON, Willie, about 10 yrs old, Plymouth.

MORGAN, Samuel R., Plymouth, wife and four children,
three of whom boys, were in the mine
and brought out dead.

SMITH, Henry, Avondale. Wife and four children. Hands
clenched as though guarding
against a blow; shirt up
around his neck; face quiet.

JONES, Thomas, Plymouth, wife and children. Buried
one child last Sunday.

ALLEN, William, Hanover, leaves
a wife, soon to be a mother.

HUGHES, Thomas, Walsh Hill, Plymouth;
face very red; arms limp; fists clenched.

EDWARDS, W. Edwards, Plymouth (Coal street); head
horribly bloated; discolored and bloody; thirty
years old. Wife and one child.

WILLIAMS, William, Hyde Park, 14 yrs
of age, who had only worked there one day

Blackdamp
from the Brooklyn Eagle New York 1902-07-12

The miners had been eating seated in groups
of five and ten, with their buckets and the remains
of their lunches scattered over the floor.

All of them were blackened. The head
of one man was crushed and the only means
of identification will be by his check number.

The arms of most of them were twisted
in front of them as if to shield
their faces from fire. The left hand of one man

was torn off at the wrist.
Outside of the property loss this catastrophe
will cost the Cambria Steel Company a large sum.

The company paid to the family of every person
killed in its employ
$1,000, and has paid every man who has lost

an eye, limb or became otherwise
partially disabled, the sum of $500.
As near as can be learned there was not one dozen

Americans killed, the rest being Huns and Slavs.
Mine Superintendent George T. Robinson
said they would have the mine ready

again for work by Monday.
At 9 o'clock this morning
there were sixteen bodies left in the morgue.

Mather Mine Gives up 63 Bodies with Known Death
List Standing at 50

Miner Rescued Alive
Wants Back
Pay with Which to Throw
Party

The Mushroom Miner
for my Mother

Under the thin, collapsing-
tunnel light, the mushrooms gleam
like knuckles. Plucked, neck-lopped, and packed

in canvas sacks, the white bulbs
softening in her hands. She loosens
every thread of root,

presses the blade
halfway down the gray-white throat
and cuts and pulls and knifes

and bags and cuts and pulls and *pulls*.
Nothing smells
like this: earth under earth, her gloved wrists

skimming potash, shit, gypsum—
soil purring
above electric heaters.

Once she finishes cleaning each rick
of mushrooms, sewing spores
back into the loam, she climbs

between the steel shunts of the lift,
unholsters her battery, lets her hard-hat
go dark.

Instinct

The coke furnace heaves with light: Roger dumps in coal,
limestone flux, iron ore, each shovelful
coughed back in sparks, orange light thrown up

for miles, and heat, such heat that Roger's sweat
turns to steam, burns off him
in blisters, softens the blue shirt he'll rip off

in the shower, where dozens of bare gray bodies
huddle like fish, the sulfur water sluicing off
him, cold. Today he'll go home

to casserole and cold cuts. Last Thursday, his wife
packed him a tuna sandwich with pickles and mustard,
her small knuckled hands dicing

through the wheezy downbeats of *Don't Explain*
when the cutting board slipped and the knife left
a jagged red seam on her thumb. She brought it

to her mouth, the penny taste of it, the comfort of blood
staying in her body. Roger remembers
that day by smell, on his lunch break

chewing his soft sandwich, taking in the fishy taste
watching cast houses where slag
oozed down, lava black, even the air

hissing with heat
when Ed Phillips tripped
over a half-filled palette

and fell onto a ream of cooling steel, glowing half-red—
how there was screaming but not
from Ed, who didn't have time when flames

tore through him, first his chest then legs then head,
the black smoke and white steam
hissing out of him. No one helped

because they couldn't.
It took three hours for the steel
to cool enough to wheel him out. The foreman tried to pull

the tar of his body free with a crowbar.
The men went home early. Roger told his wife
nothing, and by instinct Jenny knew

to make halushki and kissel, knew
to bring him to her mouth.

Made in the USA
Columbia, SC
12 April 2019